ACCOUNTABLE TIME *Journal*

Creating The **MOST** Accomplished
Version of **YOUR** Day

Hey friend!

I am thrilled you have this journal in your hands right now. This journal is the exact process I used to create over 7 figures in side gig income for myself in the last 15 years.

You can absolutely create additional income, hit a goal, start a new hobby, stay consistent with your goals and become a new person with the habits in this journal.

We will address your mindset, guiding thoughts and beliefs and actions that must happen today and tomorrow. This is not a To Do list. It's a promise you will accomplish what you need to each day. It's also not a planner. You are only focusing on today with this journal.

-- How to use this journal --

On the next page you will see descriptions of what to put in each section. I carry my journal with me in my purse and use it as a guide for my day. It's perfect for people who love electronic calendars and to do lists but still want a place to write your thoughts and beliefs and actions for today. It's also really awesome to look back every 2 months and see what you have accomplished!

THIS IS YOUR DAY.
THIS IS YOUR DREAM.
THIS IS YOUR RESPONSIBILITY.
YOU ARE NOT STUCK.
YOU ARE NOT A VICTIM.
YOU ARE NOT A LOSER.
YOU ARE NOT GOING TO QUIT.
YOU ARE A WINNER.
YOU SUCCEED.
YOU PERSEVERE.
YOU WILL NOT STOP UNTIL YOU WIN.
I BELIEVE IN YOU.
GO CRUSH IT!
XO- GRETCHEN

P.S. TAG ME ON INSTAGRAM ON YOUR WINS @GRETCHEN_HEINEN

How to Use This Journal

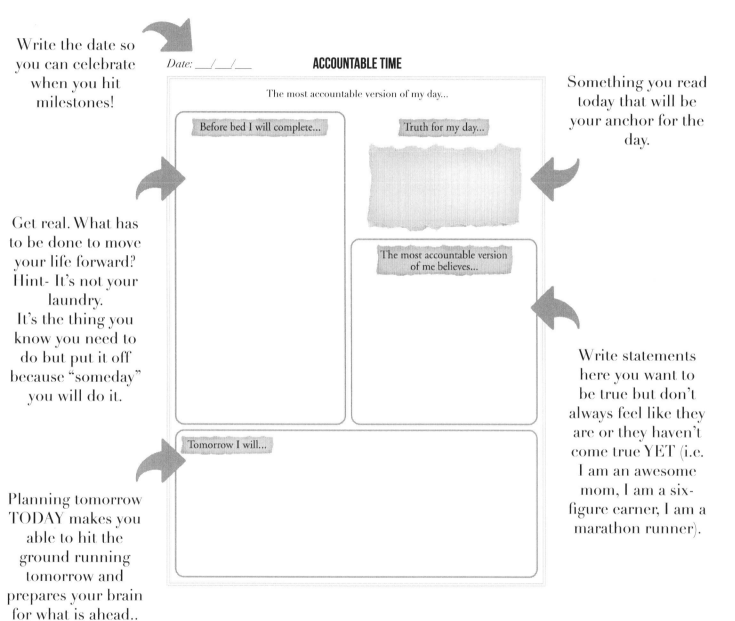

Write the date so you can celebrate when you hit milestones!

Get real. What has to be done to move your life forward? Hint- It's not your laundry.
It's the thing you know you need to do but put it off because "someday" you will do it.

Planning tomorrow TODAY makes you able to hit the ground running tomorrow and prepares your brain for what is ahead..

Something you read today that will be your anchor for the day.

Write statements here you want to be true but don't always feel like they are or they haven't come true YET (i.e. I am an awesome mom, I am a six-figure earner, I am a marathon runner).

Date: ___/___/___

ACCOUNTABLE TIME

The most accountable version of my day...

Before bed I will complete...

Truth for my day...

The most accountable version of me believes...

Tomorrow I will...

MILLIONAIRE TIP:
There is no "correct" way to journal. Just show up every day no matter how you feel. Write at least one thing in each box. Watch your life change.

Planning in Quarters

Each year is comprised of four quarters.

Q1 is January, February, March.

Q2 is April, May, June.

Q3 is July, August, September.

Q4 is October, November, December.

This journal will last you an entire quarter and I recommend starting a new one each quarter, even if you haven't finished all the pages. This way you can look back and see the progress you have made each quarter of your journey by flipping through the pages and pages of action you took.

The first page is your DREAMS LIST.

Dream big here! Put anything your heart desires. This is just a place for you to come up with possible ideas of things you want to accomplish by the end of this journal.

Your brain will use these as a guide and most of us find the "how" along the way.

The last page is your WINS LIST.

This is where you will keep a running tab of all your major wins as they happen. At the end of the quarter you will see just how far you have come.

When the quarter is over, cross check your WINS LIST with your DREAMS LIST.

It's magical to see just how far you have come. Celebrate every quarter!

RINSE AND REPEAT!

The most accountable version of my day...

Dreams List

This quarter I would like to accomplish:

ACCOUNTABLE TIME

The most accountable version of my day...

Before bed I will complete...

Truth for my day...

The most accountable version of me believes...

Tomorrow I will...

ACCOUNTABLE TIME

The most accountable version of my day...

Before bed I will complete...

Truth for my day...

The most accountable version of me believes...

Tomorrow I will...

Date: ___/___/___

ACCOUNTABLE TIME

The most accountable version of my day...

Before bed I will complete...

Truth for my day...

The most accountable version of me believes...

Tomorrow I will...

Date: ___/___/___

ACCOUNTABLE TIME

The most accountable version of my day...

Before bed I will complete...

Truth for my day...

The most accountable version of me believes...

Tomorrow I will...

ACCOUNTABLE TIME

The most accountable version of my day...

Before bed I will complete...

Truth for my day...

The most accountable version of me believes...

Tomorrow I will...

Date: ___/___/___

ACCOUNTABLE TIME

The most accountable version of my day...

Before bed I will complete...

Truth for my day...

The most accountable version
of me believes...

Tomorrow I will...

Date: ___/___/___

ACCOUNTABLE TIME

The most accountable version of my day...

Before bed I will complete...

Truth for my day...

The most accountable version of me believes...

Tomorrow I will...

Date: ___/___/___

ACCOUNTABLE TIME

The most accountable version of my day...

Before bed I will complete...

Truth for my day...

The most accountable version of me believes...

Tomorrow I will...

ACCOUNTABLE TIME

The most accountable version of my day...

Before bed I will complete...

Truth for my day...

The most accountable version of me believes...

Tomorrow I will...

ACCOUNTABLE TIME

The most accountable version of my day...

Before bed I will complete...

Truth for my day...

The most accountable version of me believes...

Tomorrow I will...

ACCOUNTABLE TIME

The most accountable version of my day...

Before bed I will complete...

Truth for my day...

The most accountable version of me believes...

Tomorrow I will...

ACCOUNTABLE TIME

The most accountable version of my day...

Before bed I will complete...

Truth for my day...

The most accountable version of me believes...

Tomorrow I will...

ACCOUNTABLE TIME

The most accountable version of my day...

Before bed I will complete...

Truth for my day...

The most accountable version of me believes...

Tomorrow I will...

Date: ___/___/___

ACCOUNTABLE TIME

The most accountable version of my day...

Before bed I will complete...

Truth for my day...

The most accountable version
of me believes...

Tomorrow I will...

ACCOUNTABLE TIME

The most accountable version of my day...

Before bed I will complete...

Truth for my day...

The most accountable version of me believes...

Tomorrow I will...

Date: ___/___/___

ACCOUNTABLE TIME

The most accountable version of my day...

Before bed I will complete...

Truth for my day...

The most accountable version of me believes...

Tomorrow I will...

ACCOUNTABLE TIME

The most accountable version of my day...

Before bed I will complete...

Truth for my day...

The most accountable version of me believes...

Tomorrow I will...

Date: ___/___/___

ACCOUNTABLE TIME

The most accountable version of my day...

Before bed I will complete...

Truth for my day...

The most accountable version
of me believes...

Tomorrow I will...

ACCOUNTABLE TIME

The most accountable version of my day...

Before bed I will complete...

Truth for my day...

The most accountable version of me believes...

Tomorrow I will...

ACCOUNTABLE TIME

The most accountable version of my day...

Before bed I will complete...

Truth for my day...

The most accountable version of me believes...

Tomorrow I will...

Date: ___/___/___

ACCOUNTABLE TIME

The most accountable version of my day...

Before bed I will complete...

Truth for my day...

The most accountable version of me believes...

Tomorrow I will...

©2020 Gretchen Heinen, All Rights Reserved

ACCOUNTABLE TIME

The most accountable version of my day...

Before bed I will complete...

Truth for my day...

The most accountable version of me believes...

Tomorrow I will...

ACCOUNTABLE TIME

The most accountable version of my day...

Before bed I will complete...

Truth for my day...

The most accountable version of me believes...

Tomorrow I will...

ACCOUNTABLE TIME

The most accountable version of my day...

Before bed I will complete...

Truth for my day...

The most accountable version of me believes...

Tomorrow I will...

ACCOUNTABLE TIME

The most accountable version of my day...

Before bed I will complete...

Truth for my day...

The most accountable version
of me believes...

Tomorrow I will...

ACCOUNTABLE TIME

The most accountable version of my day...

Before bed I will complete...

Truth for my day...

The most accountable version
of me believes...

Tomorrow I will...

Date: ___/___/___

ACCOUNTABLE TIME

The most accountable version of my day...

Before bed I will complete...

Truth for my day...

The most accountable version of me believes...

Tomorrow I will...

ACCOUNTABLE TIME

The most accountable version of my day...

Before bed I will complete...

Truth for my day...

The most accountable version of me believes...

Tomorrow I will...

ACCOUNTABLE TIME

The most accountable version of my day...

Before bed I will complete...

Truth for my day...

The most accountable version
of me believes...

Tomorrow I will...

ACCOUNTABLE TIME

The most accountable version of my day...

Before bed I will complete...

Truth for my day...

The most accountable version of me believes...

Tomorrow I will...

ACCOUNTABLE TIME

The most accountable version of my day...

Before bed I will complete...

Truth for my day...

The most accountable version of me believes...

Tomorrow I will...

Date: ___/___/___

ACCOUNTABLE TIME

The most accountable version of my day...

Before bed I will complete...

Truth for my day...

The most accountable version
of me believes...

Tomorrow I will...

ACCOUNTABLE TIME

The most accountable version of my day...

Before bed I will complete...

Truth for my day...

The most accountable version of me believes...

Tomorrow I will...

Date: ___/___/___

ACCOUNTABLE TIME

The most accountable version of my day...

Before bed I will complete...

Truth for my day...

The most accountable version of me believes...

Tomorrow I will...

ACCOUNTABLE TIME

The most accountable version of my day...

Before bed I will complete...

Truth for my day...

The most accountable version
of me believes...

Tomorrow I will...

Date: ___/___/___

ACCOUNTABLE TIME

The most accountable version of my day...

Before bed I will complete...

Truth for my day...

The most accountable version of me believes...

Tomorrow I will...

Date: ___/___/___

ACCOUNTABLE TIME

The most accountable version of my day...

Before bed I will complete...

Truth for my day...

The most accountable version
of me believes...

Tomorrow I will...

Date: ___/___/___

ACCOUNTABLE TIME

The most accountable version of my day...

Before bed I will complete...

Truth for my day...

The most accountable version of me believes...

Tomorrow I will...

Date: ___/___/___

ACCOUNTABLE TIME

The most accountable version of my day...

Before bed I will complete...

Truth for my day...

The most accountable version of me believes...

Tomorrow I will...

ACCOUNTABLE TIME

The most accountable version of my day...

Before bed I will complete...

Truth for my day...

The most accountable version of me believes...

Tomorrow I will...

ACCOUNTABLE TIME

The most accountable version of my day...

Before bed I will complete...

Truth for my day...

The most accountable version
of me believes...

Tomorrow I will...

Date: ___/___/___

ACCOUNTABLE TIME

The most accountable version of my day...

Before bed I will complete...

Truth for my day...

The most accountable version of me believes...

Tomorrow I will...

Date: ___/___/___   **ACCOUNTABLE TIME**

The most accountable version of my day...

Before bed I will complete...

Truth for my day...

The most accountable version
of me believes...

Tomorrow I will...

ACCOUNTABLE TIME

The most accountable version of my day...

Before bed I will complete...

Truth for my day...

The most accountable version
of me believes...

Tomorrow I will...

Date: ___/___/___

ACCOUNTABLE TIME

The most accountable version of my day...

Before bed I will complete...

Truth for my day...

The most accountable version of me believes...

Tomorrow I will...

ACCOUNTABLE TIME

The most accountable version of my day...

Before bed I will complete...

Truth for my day...

The most accountable version of me believes...

Tomorrow I will...

ACCOUNTABLE TIME

The most accountable version of my day...

Before bed I will complete...

Truth for my day...

The most accountable version of me believes...

Tomorrow I will...

Date: ___/___/___

ACCOUNTABLE TIME

The most accountable version of my day...

Before bed I will complete...

Truth for my day...

The most accountable version of me believes...

Tomorrow I will...

Date: ___/___/___

ACCOUNTABLE TIME

The most accountable version of my day...

Before bed I will complete...

Truth for my day...

The most accountable version of me believes...

Tomorrow I will...

Date: ___/___/___

ACCOUNTABLE TIME

The most accountable version of my day...

Before bed I will complete...

Truth for my day...

The most accountable version
of me believes...

Tomorrow I will...

ACCOUNTABLE TIME

The most accountable version of my day...

Before bed I will complete...

Truth for my day...

The most accountable version of me believes...

Tomorrow I will...

ACCOUNTABLE TIME

The most accountable version of my day...

Before bed I will complete...

Truth for my day...

The most accountable version of me believes...

Tomorrow I will...

ACCOUNTABLE TIME

The most accountable version of my day...

Before bed I will complete...

Truth for my day...

The most accountable version of me believes...

Tomorrow I will...

ACCOUNTABLE TIME

The most accountable version of my day...

Before bed I will complete...

Truth for my day...

The most accountable version of me believes...

Tomorrow I will...

ACCOUNTABLE TIME

The most accountable version of my day...

Before bed I will complete...

Truth for my day...

The most accountable version of me believes...

Tomorrow I will...

Date: ___/___/___

ACCOUNTABLE TIME

The most accountable version of my day...

Before bed I will complete...

Truth for my day...

The most accountable version
of me believes...

Tomorrow I will...

Date: ___/___/___

ACCOUNTABLE TIME

The most accountable version of my day...

Before bed I will complete...

Truth for my day...

The most accountable version
of me believes...

Tomorrow I will...

ACCOUNTABLE TIME

The most accountable version of my day...

Before bed I will complete...

Truth for my day...

The most accountable version of me believes...

Tomorrow I will...

ACCOUNTABLE TIME

The most accountable version of my day...

Before bed I will complete...

Truth for my day...

The most accountable version of me believes...

Tomorrow I will...

ACCOUNTABLE TIME

The most accountable version of my day...

Before bed I will complete...

Truth for my day...

The most accountable version
of me believes...

Tomorrow I will...

ACCOUNTABLE TIME

The most accountable version of my day...

Before bed I will complete...

Truth for my day...

The most accountable version of me believes...

Tomorrow I will...

Date: ___/___/___

The most accountable version of my day...

Before bed I will complete...

Truth for my day...

The most accountable version of me believes...

Tomorrow I will...

ACCOUNTABLE TIME

The most accountable version of my day...

Before bed I will complete...

Truth for my day...

The most accountable version of me believes...

Tomorrow I will...

ACCOUNTABLE TIME

The most accountable version of my day...

Before bed I will complete...

Truth for my day...

The most accountable version
of me believes...

Tomorrow I will...

ACCOUNTABLE TIME

The most accountable version of my day...

Before bed I will complete...

Truth for my day...

The most accountable version of me believes...

Tomorrow I will...

Date: ___/___/___

The most accountable version of my day...

Before bed I will complete...

Truth for my day...

The most accountable version of me believes...

Tomorrow I will...

Date: ___/___/___

ACCOUNTABLE TIME

The most accountable version of my day...

Before bed I will complete...

Truth for my day...

The most accountable version of me believes...

Tomorrow I will...

ACCOUNTABLE TIME

The most accountable version of my day...

Before bed I will complete...

Truth for my day...

The most accountable version of me believes...

Tomorrow I will...

ACCOUNTABLE TIME

The most accountable version of my day...

Before bed I will complete...

Truth for my day...

The most accountable version of me believes...

Tomorrow I will...

ACCOUNTABLE TIME

The most accountable version of my day...

Before bed I will complete...

Truth for my day...

The most accountable version of me believes...

Tomorrow I will...

ACCOUNTABLE TIME

The most accountable version of my day...

Before bed I will complete...

Truth for my day...

The most accountable version
of me believes...

Tomorrow I will...

ACCOUNTABLE TIME

The most accountable version of my day...

Before bed I will complete...

Truth for my day...

The most accountable version of me believes...

Tomorrow I will...

Date: ___/___/___

ACCOUNTABLE TIME

The most accountable version of my day...

Before bed I will complete...

Truth for my day...

The most accountable version of me believes...

Tomorrow I will...

ACCOUNTABLE TIME

The most accountable version of my day...

Before bed I will complete...

Truth for my day...

The most accountable version of me believes...

Tomorrow I will...

ACCOUNTABLE TIME

The most accountable version of my day...

Before bed I will complete...

Truth for my day...

The most accountable version
of me believes...

Tomorrow I will...

Date: ___/___/___

ACCOUNTABLE TIME

The most accountable version of my day...

Before bed I will complete...

Truth for my day...

The most accountable version of me believes...

Tomorrow I will...

ACCOUNTABLE TIME

The most accountable version of my day...

Before bed I will complete...

Truth for my day...

The most accountable version of me believes...

Tomorrow I will...

ACCOUNTABLE TIME

Date: ___/___/___

The most accountable version of my day...

Before bed I will complete...

Truth for my day...

The most accountable version
of me believes...

Tomorrow I will...

ACCOUNTABLE TIME

The most accountable version of my day...

Before bed I will complete...

Truth for my day...

The most accountable version of me believes...

Tomorrow I will...

ACCOUNTABLE TIME

The most accountable version of my day...

Before bed I will complete...

Truth for my day...

The most accountable version of me believes...

Tomorrow I will...

Date: ___/___/___

ACCOUNTABLE TIME

The most accountable version of my day...

Before bed I will complete...

Truth for my day...

The most accountable version of me believes...

Tomorrow I will...

ACCOUNTABLE TIME

The most accountable version of my day...

Before bed I will complete...

Truth for my day...

The most accountable version of me believes...

Tomorrow I will...

Date: ___ /___ /___

The most accountable version of my day...

Before bed I will complete...

Truth for my day...

The most accountable version
of me believes...

Tomorrow I will...

ACCOUNTABLE TIME

The most accountable version of my day...

Before bed I will complete...

Truth for my day...

The most accountable version of me believes...

Tomorrow I will...

ACCOUNTABLE TIME

The most accountable version of my day...

Before bed I will complete...

Truth for my day...

The most accountable version of me believes...

Tomorrow I will...

Date: ___/___/___

ACCOUNTABLE TIME

The most accountable version of my day...

Before bed I will complete...

Truth for my day...

The most accountable version of me believes...

Tomorrow I will...

Date: ___/___/___

ACCOUNTABLE TIME

The most accountable version of my day...

Before bed I will complete...

Truth for my day...

The most accountable version of me believes...

Tomorrow I will...

ACCOUNTABLE TIME

The most accountable version of my day...

Before bed I will complete...

Truth for my day...

The most accountable version of me believes...

Tomorrow I will...

ACCOUNTABLE TIME

The most accountable version of my day...

Before bed I will complete...

Truth for my day...

The most accountable version of me believes...

Tomorrow I will...

Date: ___/___/___

ACCOUNTABLE TIME

The most accountable version of my day...

Before bed I will complete...

Truth for my day...

The most accountable version
of me believes...

Tomorrow I will...

ACCOUNTABLE TIME

The most accountable version of my day...

Before bed I will complete...

Truth for my day...

The most accountable version of me believes...

Tomorrow I will...

End Date: ___/___/___   **ACCOUNTABLE TIME**   *Q: 1 2 3 4 (Circle One)*

The most accountable version of my day...

Wins List

Write your answers inside this box.

The most accountable version of my day...

You did it!!!!!!!

I hope you are insanely proud of yourself.

Next steps:

Grab your next Accountable Time Journal on Amazon

Listen to the episodes on Accountable Time on the Net Worth It Podcast

gretchenheinen.com/podcast

(Available on most podcast readers)

Keep going!

Made in the USA
Monee, IL
04 January 2022

87836662R00055